L I B R A R Y   O F   C O N G R E S S

Africana Collections

A N   I L L U S T R A T E D   G U I D E

L I B R A R Y   O F   C O N G R E S S   W A S H I N G T O N   2 0 0 1

Written by Joanne M. Zellers, African area specialist in the African Section, under the general guidance of Beverly Gray, chief of the African and Middle Eastern Division, with contributions from the author's knowledgeable colleagues in the African Section: Angel Batiste, Marieta L. Harper, and Mattye Laverne Page. Special thanks to Joan Higbee, Hispanic Division, who suggested illustrations from several special format collections, and to Evelyn Sinclair of the Publishing Office for her invaluable advice and inspired editing. These cooperative efforts have improved the content of this guide and are gratefully acknowledged.

COVER: Purchased in Bangui, Central African Republic, in 1981, this example of an art form popular in West and Central Africa is designed in a geometric pattern. Butterfly wings in an abundant variety of colors are gathered by local artists who also fashion from them images of people, animals, or domestic rural scenes. *(African and Middle Eastern Division)*

This publication was made possible by generous support from the James Madison Council, a national, private-sector advisory council dedicated to helping the Library of Congress share its unique resources with the nation and the world.

Africana Collections is composed in Centaur, a typeface designed by American typographer and book designer Bruce Rogers (1870–1957). The full type font was first used at the Montague Press in 1915 for an edition of Maurice de Guerin's *The Centaur*.

This guide was designed by Robert L. Wiser, Archetype Press, Inc., Washington, D.C.

Copies of illustrations that have been photographed from items in the Library's collections may be ordered through the Photoduplication Service, Library of Congress, Washington, DC 20540-4570. Copyright restrictions will apply.

LIBRARY OF CONGRESS CATALOGING-IN-PUBLICATION DATA

Library of Congress.
    Library of Congress Africana collections : an illustrated guide.
        p.   cm.   — (Library of Congress African and Middle Eastern collections illustrated guides)
    Text by Joanne M. Zellers.
    Includes bibliographical references.
    ISBN 0-8444-1041-1
    1. Africa, Sub-Saharan—Library resources. 2. Library of Congress. African Section. 3. Africa, Sub-Saharan—Library resources.—Pictorial works. 4. Library of Congress. African Section—Pictorial works. I. Zellers, Joanne M. II. Title. III. Title: Africana collections. IV. Series: Library of Congress. Library of Congress African and Middle Eastern collections illustrated guides.
Z3501.L53 2001
[DT351]
026'.967—dc21
        2001016514

For sale by the U.S. Government Printing Office
Superintendent of Documents
Mail Stop: SSOP, Washington, DC 20402-9328

Contents

Foreword

THE AFRICAN AND MIDDLE EASTERN DIVISION (AMED) was created in 1978 as part of a general Library of Congress reorganization. At that time, three disparate administrative units—the African Section, the Near East Section, and the Hebraic Section—were combined. Together they cover some seventy countries and regions from Southern Africa to the Maghreb and from the Middle East to Central Asia. The division coordinates and directs the component sections. Each section plays a vital role in the Library's acquisitions program; offers expert reference and bibliographic services to Congress and researchers in this country and abroad; develops projects, special events, and publications; and cooperates and participates with other institutions and scholarly and professional associations in the United States and around the world.

Although proposed earlier, it was not until 1960—with mounting national academic and government interest in sub-Saharan Africa—that the Library's African Section was established, administered initially by the General Reference and Bibliography Division. This section focuses on virtually all topics relating to sub-Saharan Africa. In 1945, the Near East Section had been created as part of the Orientalia Division to serve as a focal point of the Library's programs for this pivotal area, which includes North Africa, the Arab world, Turkey, Iran, the Caucasus, Central Asia, and Islam. The Hebraic Section, the oldest of the three, began operation in 1914 as part of the Division of Semitic and Oriental Literature, and it concentrates on Jewish culture, Israel, the Hebrew language, biblical studies, and the ancient Near East.

Volumes about Africa and the Middle East were among the books making up one of the first major purchases by the Library of Congress, the 1815 acquisition of Thomas Jefferson's library, the subject and linguistic range of which greatly influenced future Library acquisition policies. Although sporadic receipts of publications from or about the region were reported in various annual reports of the Librarian of Congress over the years, systematic acquisition efforts for publications from this part of the world were limited before World War II. Yet today the African and Middle Eastern Division is recognized as a major world resource center for Africa, the Middle East, the Caucasus, and Central Asia.

The Hebraic and Near East sections have custody of materials in many formats in the non-roman-alphabet languages of the region, which together number more than half a million volumes. The Hebraic Section collections contain some 160,000 volumes in Hebrew and related languages, including Yiddish, Ladino, Syriac, and the languages of Ethiopia. Materials in more than forty languages are held by the Near East Section, the major holdings of which are

Ẹ̀kpè Okonkọ

in Arabic (the largest language group represented, with approximately 130,000 volumes), Persian, Turkish, non-Cyrillic Central Asian languages, Armenian, and Georgian. Although the African Section has no formal custodial responsibilities, it maintains a pamphlet collection of more than 22,000 items.

To further enhance holdings already strong in the fields of history, literature, economics, linguistics, art, religion, and philosophical studies, division curators participate in acquiring materials of research value through purchase, copyright, exchange, and gift. Noteworthy grants and gifts have also served to strengthen these collections. For example, in 1960 a grant from the Carnegie Corporation provided initial support for the African Section, including staff travel to many African countries to obtain publications for the Library's collections. Gifts from Jacob H. Schiff, one in 1912 and another in 1914, enabled the Library to acquire nearly 10,000

Ẹ̀kpè Okonkọ, a watercolor sketch, ca. 1930, by Ibo artist D. L. K. Nnachy, depicts a dance celebrating the harvest of new yams. Nnachy was born about 1910 in the Ohafia area of eastern Nigeria. Twenty-two of his watercolors are among the papers of the Harmon Foundation (see page 20). (*Reproduced by courtesy of the Harmon Foundation*) (*Manuscript Division*)

7

Iri-Agha, a watercolor by D. L. K. Nnachy, ca. 1930, shows a drummer, a horn-player, singers, and dancers who carry a board decorated with wooden skulls and human heads. Nnachy's sketches, applications from many other African artists seeking foundation support, biographical information, awards, scrapbooks, and administrative files are found in the Harmon Foundation Papers. *(Reproduced by courtesy of the Harmon Foundation) (Manuscript Division)*

volumes and substantially increased the Hebraica collections. Generous gifts from Mr. and Mrs. Arthur Dadian in the 1990s created an endowment to develop and maintain the Library's Armenian holdings.

In the spring of 1997, the division moved from the John Adams Building to its present imposing location in the newly renovated Thomas Jefferson Building. The new African and Middle Eastern Division Reading Room houses a 10,000-volume reference collection and a rotating display of current events journals, arranged and maintained by each of the three sections. The division welcomes visitors and provides prearranged briefings on its activities and services for individuals and for groups. Researchers may consult specialists who readily provide in-depth reference assistance in identifying materials in their custodial collection as well as related sources about Africa, the Middle East, the Caucasus, and Central Asia in roman script and in other formats or specializations found in the Library of Congress General Collections or in units such as the Geography and Map Division, the Manuscript Division, the Rare Book and Special Collections Division, and the Law Library.

In the several display cases located in its grand reading room, the division mounts small exhibits such as *Oil and Petroleum in Africa and the Middle East.* Major exhibits featuring AMED collections have been mounted in the Library's galleries. *From the Ends of the Earth: Judaic Treasures of the Library of Congress* was prepared to mark the seventy-fifth anniversary of the Hebraic Section, and a version of this exhibit later traveled to several North American cities.

Special events and outreach activities have long been part of the division's agenda. Working through the three sections, it sponsors many library, cultural, and scholarly programs. The Africana Librarians Council of the African Studies Association has held several of its semiannual meetings at the Library. Officials of the International Summer Seminar in Jewish Genealogy accepted an offer from the Hebraic Section to serve as host for the seminar's 1995 meeting, making the Library's outstanding genealogy-related resources readily available to participants. As part of its fiftieth anniversary celebration in 1995, the Near East Section held a conference on "Arab-American Cultural Relations," and more recently, it cosponsored with the Embassy of Tunisia a panel of international experts who spoke on "Tunisia: Past, Present, and Future." Lectures, including a research seminar series, are another important and ongoing part of the division's outreach program. Well-known speakers such as MacArthur Fellow and human rights lawyer Gay McDougall, Nobel Laureate Elie Wiesel, and Egyptian philosopher Zaki Naguib Mahmoud have participated.

Another role of the division is to facilitate projects to enhance access to the collections, as it does through the widely acclaimed body of publications issued under its auspices. The African Section has compiled more than forty publications ranging from bibliographies of official publications of African nations to short subject guides on contemporary issues such as *Abuja: The New Federal Capital of Nigeria*. Titles prepared in the Near East Section include *The Holy Koran at the Library of Congress* and *American Doctoral Dissertations on the Arab World*. The catalog of the highly successful exhibit initiated by the Hebraic Section, *Scrolls from the Dead Sea: The Ancient Library of Qumran and Modern Scholarship*, published jointly by the Library and the Israel Antiquities Authority, received several awards for its design.

The African and Middle Eastern Division continues to exert a vital influence in the development of area studies librarianship. Its staff is recognized for scholarly publications. They serve as officers in area studies organizations and attend and participate in national and international meetings on their areas of expertise. And, finally, a significant contribution made by the division is in its training of young scholars and future librarians through briefings and presentations, the internships and volunteer positions it offers, and the mentoring it provides to promising candidates, thus preparing the way for the future success of the study of these vital areas in world culture.

BEVERLY GRAY
CHIEF, AFRICAN AND MIDDLE EASTERN DIVISION

Frank G. Carpenter (1855–1924), an American journalist and photographer, visited numerous regions of Africa in 1881, 1886, 1906–7, and 1908–9, where he and his daughter assembled extensive photographic files to document and illustrate his books. As a collector of photographs, Carpenter showed a wide breadth of interests in the diversity of daily life across the African continent. "Africa, Native Girl, 1900," photographed by C. Vincent of Dar-es-Salaam, Tanzania, and "Zanzibar Sultan" are examples of work in his collections. In 1951, his daughter, Frances Carpenter, gave the Library this important visual resource. The Frank and Frances Carpenter collection includes approximately 5,600 original contact prints, 8,000 negatives, and a large group of gold-toned albumen prints from commercial firms. *(Prints and Photographs Division)*

THE
ROYAL AFRICAN:
OR,
MEMOIRS
OF THE
Young Prince of *Annamaboe*.

Comprehending

A diſtinct Account of his Country and Family; his elder Brother's Voyage to *France,* and Reception there; the Manner in which himſelf was confided by his Father to the Captain who ſold him; his Condition while a Slave in *Barbadoes*; the true Cauſe of his being redeemed; his Voyage from thence; and Reception here in *England.*

Interſpers'd throughout

With ſeveral HISTORICAL REMARKS on the Commerce of the *European* Nations, whoſe Subjects frequent the Coaſt of *Guinea.*

To which is prefixed

A LETTER from the AUTHOR to a Perſon of Diſtinction, in Reference to ſome natural Curioſities in *Africa*; as well as explaining the Motives which induced him to compoſe theſe MEMOIRS.

Othello ſhews the Muſe's utmoſt Power,
A brave, an honeſt, yet a hapleſs Moor.
In *Oroonoko* ſhines the Hero's Mind,
With native Luſtre by no Art refin'd.
Sweet *Juba* ſtrikes us but with milder Charms,
At once renown'd for Virtue, Love, and Arms.
Yet hence might riſe a ſtill more moving Tale,
But *Shakeſpears, Addiſons,* and *Southerns* fail!

LONDON: Printed for W. REEVE, at *Shakeſpear's Head, Fleetſtreet*; G. WOODFALL, and J. BARNES, at *Charing-Croſs*; and at the Court of Requeſts.

(1750)

Introduction

THE AFRICANA COLLECTIONS OF THE LIBRARY OF CONGRESS include materials produced over the centuries by peoples living in sub-Saharan Africa and by others inspired by the continent. Encompassing the area from the Cape Verde Islands in the west to the Indian Ocean islands in the east and from the Sahel in the north to the Cape of Good Hope in the south, this geographic region of fifty countries spanning several climatic zones, whose peoples speak hundreds of languages, offers rich opportunities for diverse studies. The Library's Africana collections reflect the complexities of African societies and the efforts to understand and express this knowledge in many forms. This guide highlights some of these holdings of materials created in Africa or about it.

Those who have just begun their studies as well as experienced scholars will find in the Africana collections pertinent books, periodicals, newspapers, pamphlets, legal documents, photographs, films, music, sound recordings, and CD-ROMs. The Library's collections cover all subjects except technical agriculture and clinical medicine. These materials are stored in the General Collections and in the Library's various custodial divisions as their format dictates. Reference assistance in locating and using them is available from the African Section. Established in 1960 with support from the Carnegie Corporation of New York, the African Section is the focal point of the Library's collection development, reference, and bibliographic activities for sub-Saharan Africa. In addition to fulfilling its mandate to provide reference services for Congress, the American people, and the international community, the African Section maintains liaisons with other institutions in the United States and abroad. Each African Section professional staff member has reference and acquisitions responsibilities for a particular linguistic or geographic region and has developed expert knowledge of the collections for his or her area. In conjunction with other Library units, the section develops the collections and compiles bibliographic guides to bring Africana materials to the attention of librarians and scholars.

The African Section has prepared numerous studies for publication, ranging from general and topical guides on sub-Saharan Africa to bibliographies of official publications of a country or region, some of which are cited in "Selected Library of Congress Publications on Africa." The purpose of each is to open up the collections, to make them more accessible, and to increase the number of people who may benefit from exploring these Africana treasures.

JOANNE M. ZELLERS
AREA SPECIALIST FOR AFRICA, AFRICAN SECTION

OPPOSITE. Materials in the various custodial divisions of the Library of Congress complement one another. In *The Royal African* (1750), purportedly the memoirs of an African man enslaved at the Annamaboe fort, the author describes the architecture of the fort and its role in local commerce and governance in the Gold Coast, West Africa. (*Rare Book and Special Collections Division*)

BELOW. A detail of a manuscript map based on a survey completed in February or March 1756 by G. Justly Watson shows the fort at about the same time. Both this map and the memoirs pictured opposite are invaluable resources to historians. (*Geography and Map Division*)

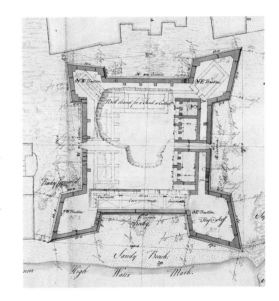

Overview

NUSUALLY RICH AND EXTENSIVE RESEARCH MATERIALS concerning the fifty countries of sub-Saharan Africa, an area that includes the Western Indian Ocean Islands but excludes the North African countries of Algeria, Egypt, Libya, Morocco, and Tunisia, are available at the Library of Congress. The Library's collections of Africana—material from or relating to Africa—are among the best in the world. Although most Africa-related material is dispersed in the Library's general book and periodical collections, impressive works of Africana may also be found in the collections of manuscripts, maps, microforms, music, newspapers, prints, photographs, and films in the various special-format custodial divisions of the Library. Every major field of study except technical agriculture and clinical medicine is represented. Holdings in economics, history, linguistics, and literature are especially strong.

The Library has a longstanding role in acquiring and providing access to material about Africa, beginning with the Thomas Jefferson collection purchased in 1815, which included several books on Africa. The Library has developed one of the world's outstanding collections by acquiring and retaining materials through copyright deposit, by purchase, by the exchange of publications, and by encouraging collectors or creators of Africana to donate their treasures to an institution pledged to preserve them for future generations.

The growth of the collections over the years has been phenomenal. According to the *Annual Report of the Librarian of Congress* of 1901, the Library's collection of materials about the entire continent of Africa included about 1,830 volumes and 78 pamphlets. Measuring the largest single block of material in the General Collections, that is, surveys, yearbooks, histories, and general descriptive works under the DT classification, as an example, in 1960 the Library held about 13,000 books and periodicals in this category alone, in 1970 it held 21,000, and in 1997 it counted 50,000. The African Section's Pamphlet Collection currently numbers more than 22,000 items, among them brochures, speeches, conference papers, and other ephemera.

The Library's field offices in Nairobi, Kenya, which obtains materials from Eastern, Central, and Southern Africa and the Indian Ocean islands and that in Cairo, Egypt, whose acquisition responsibilities include Mauritania and Sudan, have been instrumental during the last thirty years in developing one of the most extensive collections of contemporary materials published in sub-Saharan Africa. These field offices manage networks of bibliographic representatives resident in each of twenty-eight countries in Central, Eastern, and Southern Africa who make contact with any organization likely to issue publications. Because of small press

CAPE TOWN.

December 1831.

This 1870 map of the Liberian coast is one of many maps of the American Colonization Society that form a special collection in the Geography and Map Division. It is estimated that the society assisted about six thousand former slaves between 1820 and 1867 to settle in what was to become Liberia. This map of Liberia is available on the Internet through the Library's Web site. *(Geography and Map Division)*

runs, on-the-spot collecting of African publications has been crucial to the successful assembling of unparalleled resources in contemporary African imprints.

A number of gifts of manuscripts and special collections are highlighted in this guide. Organizations and individuals have also deposited collections of archives, correspondence, photographs, maps, posters, and memorabilia in the Library of Congress. Of special note is the American Colonization Society collection, a key research source for scholars of Liberian history and related topics, which provides primary data on the society and its work in founding that country. Particularly important are the American Colonization Society manuscript records that are housed in the Manuscript Division and the photographs from the collection, which are located in the Prints and Photographs Division.

From ancient hand-drawn charts to the latest satellite surveys, the Geography and Map Division houses more than 150,000 maps and atlases of Africa offering diverse types of information, including political and geographic divisions, environmental conditions, and ethnological data. Besides the illustrations that may be found in journals and books from the General Collections and in the Rare Book and Special Collections Division, many images of Africa may be found in the Prints and Photographs Division and the Motion Picture, Broadcasting, and Recorded Sound Division. The Library offers the researcher the opportunity to hear the sounds of Africa in the Performing Arts Reading Room or in the Folklife Reading Room, housing the Archive of Folk Culture.

Preserving its collections is one of the Library's basic functions. In addition to an active conservation program, the Library investigates the best way to store the information contained in these materials, whether by the acquisition of facsimile or reprint editions or by transfer to microformat or electronic storage. The Library of Congress seeks to offer researchers what is needed in Africana today and to acquire and preserve what will be needed in the centuries to come.

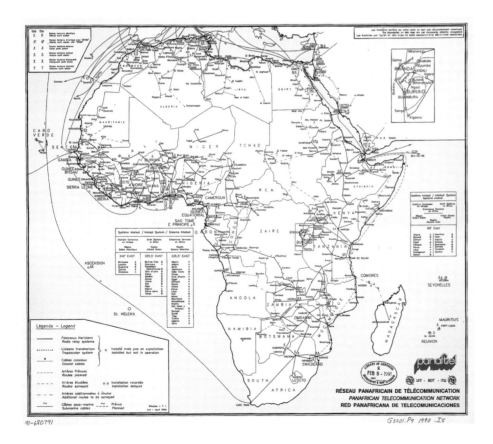

The telecommunications industry and other new technologies are key to the continuing development of African economies. This map, *Reseau panafricain de télécommunication = Panafrican telecommunication network = Red panafricana de telecommunicaciones*, produced by the International Telecommunications Union, offers a graphic depiction of these resources as of April 1990. (*Geography and Map Division*)

Creative Expression, Culture, and Society

THE CREATIVE EXPRESSIONS OF AFRICAN PEOPLES are a complex blend of many media, each of which offers a unique perspective and which together communicate everything from the mundane to the sublime. The collections of the Library of Congress are particularly strong in information about art, handicrafts, music, dance, film, oral and written literatures, and other aspects of the humanities that enrich life in each African community and which have influenced societies wherever peoples of African descent have settled.

Celebrations of African arts have drawn international audiences. Brochures, commemorative programs, conference papers, films, music, and sound recordings document these events. The first World Black and African Festival of Arts and Culture (FESTAC), for instance, was held in Dakar in 1966 and the second in Lagos in 1977. FESPACO (Festival panafricain du cinéma de Ouagadougou) which began in 1969 as result of FESTAC, 1966, is held every two years in the capital city of Burkina Faso. It gathers together all elements of the African motion picture industry to view the best the industry has to offer and to award prizes. The Library has been successful in acquiring the organization's quarterly *FESPACO Newsletter*, individual monographs, every festival's program, and many related materials such as posters.

In Africa, Anansi the Spider was a god, of the sort easily demoted by missionary theology to the rank of demon or imp: a spirit of ruses, deceits and evasions, of compulsive activity unimpeded by ethics. Abducted by slave traders and shipped to the Caribbean, he there developed as a folklore character, the not-always-successful mover of hard-nosed comic and satirical tales whose tellers would habitually close with the disingenuously polite formula, 'Jack Mantora, me no choose none'—'Mr Listener, don't think I'm getting at *you*'.

In these stories, Anansi still speaks with a shaman's spirit voice, high and hoarse, and in a dishevelled language that's a travesty of whatever dialect he might be supposed to use. But in his rural setting populated by creatures with suggestively human habits, he's usually more of a man than a spider. Indeed, the spider-guise is only a partial fit for what he is: the mixture of trap-setting and opportunism is there, but he lacks the patient, broadly-engineered strategy of the female spinner of webs. Not the best of fits; but good enough for Anansi to keep bluffing his way along with, so long as he can get away with it. Like any showman, he needs to stay in business.

Jack Mantora, me no choose none.

RIGHT. A relief panel from Benin is shown in one of thirty-five color transparencies of African sculpture produced by Art Council Aids (ca. 1953). From the collection of Mr. and Mrs. William T. Pearson, the sculpture exhibits a style based on the distinctive appliquéd textiles for which the kingdom of Abomey is well known. This series of slides is one example of the resources available to assist in the teaching of African studies. *(Prints and Photographs Division)*

OPPOSITE. Kente cloth is the name for the woven textiles produced by strip weaving by the masters of this technique, the Ashanti and Ewe peoples of West Africa. Designs were created specifically for royalty, for the wealthy, and for ceremonial occasions, and the status and gender of the wearer of each cloth was proclaimed to all those who saw it and understood the meanings conveyed by color and design. Illustrated, from *African Majesty: The Textile Art of the Ashanti and the Ewe* (New York: Thames and Hudson, 1992) by Peter Adler and Nicholas Barnard, are a cloth intended for wear by a woman and one for a man to wear. *(Illustrations copyright © 1992 by Peter Adler. Courtesy Peter Adler Gallery, London) (General Collections)*

These may be found in the General Collections, in the African Section's pamphlet collection, and in the Motion Picture, Broadcasting, and Recorded Sound Division.

Exhibition catalogs assist art collectors, art historians, anthropologists and others to authenticate early works and to trace the evolution of African art. For example, the catalog for the New York Museum of Modern Art exhibition *African Negro Art* (1935) documents its innovative emphasis on the artistry of the works included rather than on their "exotic" origins. Catalogs often provide the context, explain the function, and trace the development of artistic expression. The Library's collection of hundreds of studies of graphic designs and textiles in books and periodicals such as *African Arts* and *Arts d'Afrique noire* have assisted both academic researchers and commercial artists.

Information about artists and art collections may be found in sources such as the Harmon Foundation collection of 37,600 items housed in the Manuscript Division. Among its files of correspondence, catalogs, and scrapbooks are biographical notes on African artists and correspondence between the foundation and African art centers, publishers, and artists. In the Performing Arts Reading Room are monographs with recordings such as *Art et artisanat tsogho* (1975), including interviews with Mitsogho artisans of Gabon.

Of the four hundred to one thousand languages spoken in Africa, the Library of Congress tries to collect materials in as many African languages as there are materials published or recorded, including "contact" languages (that is, creoles and pidgins). The Library collects studies about the evolution and special

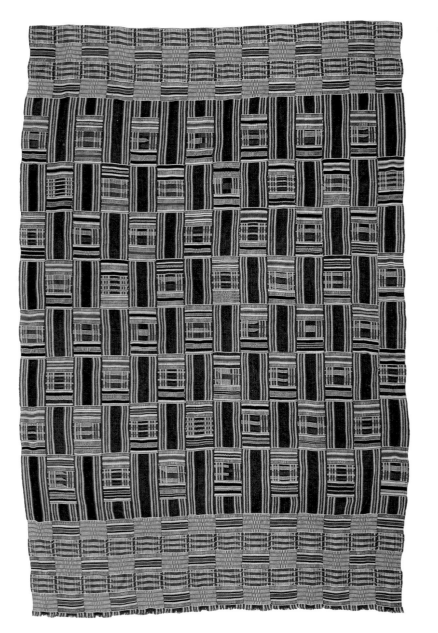

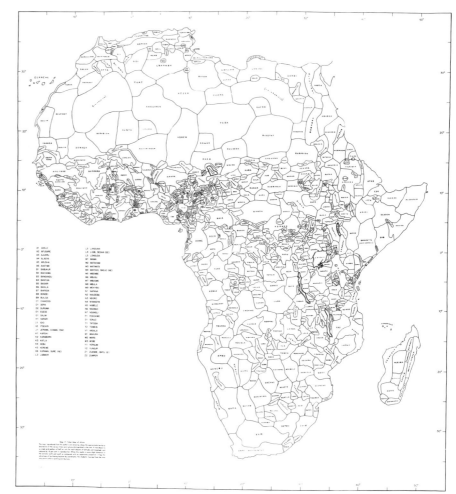

TOP LEFT. Cloth stamped with Adinkra symbols, popular today as commercial or organizational logos, has been worn in Africa to express personal theological or philosophical beliefs. In his *The Language of Adinkra Patterns* (Legon, Ghana: Sebewie Ventures, 1972; 1994), Alfred Kofi Quarcoo offers a table of symbols. *(General Collections)*

TOP RIGHT. The African continent glories in diversity. Based on his own drawing, this map by George P. Murdock from his *Africa. Its Peoples and Their Culture History* (1959) shows hundreds of ethnic groups. *(Copyright © 1959 by the McGraw-Hill Book Company, Inc.) (General Collections and African and Middle Eastern Division Reading Room)*

characteristics of European languages as spoken outside the country of origin (for instance, French as spoken in Côte d'Ivoire). Although most African languages use either a modified roman or the Arabic alphabet, others, such as Ge'ez in Ethiopia or Vai in Liberia, developed independently. All alphabets are represented in the Library's collections. The *Language Map of Africa and the Adjacent Islands*, published in 1977 on four sheets with a text and index, graphically portrays the diversity and complexity of African languages.

The Library's outstanding collections of dictionaries, grammars, and similar linguistic studies are well known published materials. Other studies are rare manuscripts. "Breves notas para o diccionaro N'bundo ou Angolense," a manuscript dictionary dated ca. 1883 is held in the Manuscript Division. Others appear in more than one format, such as *Bibliographie des langues camerounaises* (1993), a book accompanied by a computer disk.

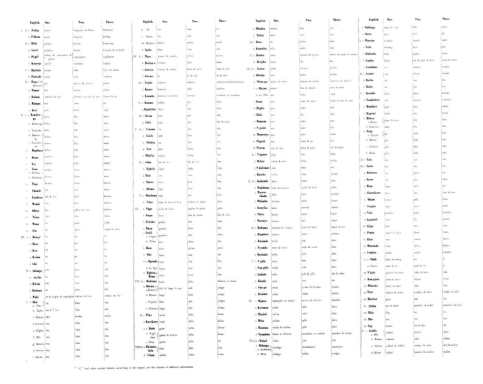

The table shown is from Sigismund Koelle's *Polyglotta Africana*, containing columns of English words with corresponding vocabulary in multiple African languages, organized in grouped sections labeled with Roman numerals and letters.

The *Yoruba Collection of William & Berta Bascom, University of California, Berkeley* (1993), consisting of about 700 microfiches, reproduces a collection of 470 rare books mainly on the Yoruba language but also features biographies, novels, hymnals, literary criticism, folklore, and histories, by various authors, dated from 1841 to 1973, held in the Bancroft Library at the University of California, Berkeley. The works are chiefly in Yoruba with some volumes in English, French, Hausa, and Latin. This compilation is available in the Microform Reading Room.

Languages may also be studied using the Library's collections of recordings of the spoken word, music, and films. *La Crotte tenace et autres contes ngbaka-ma'bo de République centrafricaine* (1975) combines music, poetry, songs, and tales from the Central African Republic in a book and two sound discs. The compilers describe it as a "a collection of 13 texts corresponding to nine Ngbaka-ma'bo tales and songtales, two of which were obtained in several versions. For each text in Ngbaka (with phonological transcription) there are three corresponding stages of translation: one, word for word, a translation in intelligible French, and a final translation" (p. 7). This work provides summaries in English, French, German, Russian, and Spanish.

The Library offers the researcher the opportunity to hear the sounds of Africa in the Performing Arts Reading Room or in the Folklife Reading Room, where the Archive of Folk Culture is housed. A wide spectrum of music and sound recordings is represented, including contemporary music; traditional music such as that associated with specific ceremonies or events including weddings or funerals; songs and ballads written for political parties and protest movements; and national anthems.

The recording *Bantu Music from British East Africa* (1954) provides a map indicating the location of each recording and descriptions and photographs of the musical instruments used. *African Rhythm: A Northern Ewe Perspective* (1995), a study about the Ewes living in Ghana and their music, includes a sound disc. In addition to their performance value, musical instruments may be works of art in themselves. In *Musical Instruments of Africa: Their Nature, Use, and Place in the Life of a Deeply Musical People* (1965), the visual and functional aspects of instruments are explored in the printed text and on a phonodisc.

The Library's collections of hymnals have been used by theologians, linguists, and musicians. Among the many owned by the Library is *Incwadi yamagama* (1849), a Zulu hymnal compiled by the American Zulu Mission, which is bound with a Zulu catechism *Incwadi yokubuza: inhliziyo yako ma i bambe amazi ami* (1849), the latter containing Bible questions and answers, the Ten Commandments, and the Lord's Prayer. These works are found in the Rare Book and Special Collections Division.

Materials about music and musicians may be found in several other divisions. For author, educator, and poet Melvin Beaunorus Tolson (1900–1966), the Manuscript Division holds a collection of his papers (1932–75, the bulk of which date from 1940 to 1966), about 4,000 items that document his activities, which ranged from serving as mayor of Langston, Oklahoma, to becoming poet laureate of Liberia. His *Libretto for the Republic of Liberia* (1953) is in the Rare Book and Special Collections Division.

Those interested in dance studies, linguistics, or cultural anthropology may view videos in the Motion Picture, Broadcasting, and Recorded Sound Division. *Cultural Dances*, produced for the Kaduna State Council for Arts and Culture in Nigeria (1990?), is a video recording in Hausa showing costumed performances. The video recording of the coronation of the Kabaka of the Buganda, Ronald Mutebi (Mutebi II), *Empaka za' maato emunyonyo* (1993), shows a three-stage ceremony reflecting both traditional customs and contemporary political administration of interest to historians, political scientists, and anthropologists. A similar documentary produced by Universal Pictures, *Haile Selassie — Coronation Festivities,*

OPPOSITE. This Senufo wall hanging from Korhogo in northern Côte d'Ivoire consists of six strips of cotton cloth that have been sewn together, commonly called a fila cloth. The geometric designs and realistic figures drawn on the cloth by Senufo religious artists are traditionally used to communicate to the gods and to the participants in Poro society ceremonies the wearer's desire for protection and for life's necessities. Widely imitated and replicated, Senufo paintings are sold all over the continent as mass-produced tourist art. (*African and Middle Eastern Division*)

Written in Ge'ez, the liturgical language of the Ethiopian Orthodox Christian Church, on parchment, *The Psalm of David*, *Ge'ez Manuscript Psalter* dates from the fifteenth or sixteenth century. The psalter refers to the Holy Trinity, Mary, Jonah, Zachariah, and others. Depicted here is Moses receiving the tablets of the Law. *(Hebraic Section)*

Bound in goat skin leather, the Islamic prayer book *Fī Madḥ Al-Rasūl* has an inscription that dates its creation to before 1894 in the Gambia. This beautiful manuscript is written in Arabic with local language translations. *(Near East Section)*

1930 includes close-ups of the Ethiopian and western dignitaries in attendance as well as views of Addis Ababa, particularly its large, open-air market and its artisans at work.

The oral narrative, whether epic poetry, folktale, or recitation of a historic event, may be presented by a storyteller, with dramatic emphasis and artistic skill before a live audience. The narrator's performance is sometimes accompanied by music and costumed dancers. Transcriptions of individual epics and griot recordings, such as *La Geste de Ségou* (1979), tell stories like this one about the medieval kingdom of Segu (Mali). Here the tale is recited by Bambara griots and recorded on disc and also transcribed as text. Anthologies such as *Oral Epics from Africa: Vibrant Voices from a Vast Continent* (1997) present a selection of works from across the continent. Also available are video recordings such as *Keita: The Heritage of the Griot* (1994), which dramatizes the Malian epic describing the life of Soundiata Keita, king of Mali (A.D. ca. 1211–55). Modern African poets, novelists, and dramatists have drawn on the classic tales, proverbs, and histories of their communities.

The Library's collections include first editions, reprints, and translations of such African authors as Amos Tutuola, Camara Laye, Chinua Achebe, Cyprian Ekwensi, Ayi Kwei Armah, and Elechi Amadi, to name just a few. The Library's collections of literary journals, such as *Présence Africaine* and *Black Orpheus*, and African newspapers that publish poetry and other literary works will interest researchers.

The Library is proud to count in its collections such ground-breaking works as Maxamed Daahir Afrax's *Maana-Faay: qiso* (1981–91), reportedly the first novel written in romanized Somali script and Abdulai Sila's *Eterna paixão* (1994), said to be the first novel published in Guinea-Bissau after it achieved independence from Portugal. The Library owns the 1968 and 1970 editions of *The Black Hermit*, by Ngũgĩ wa Thiong'o, reputedly the first full-length play by an East African author. The works of the three African authors who have won the Nobel Prize for Literature, Wole Soyinka (Nigeria) in 1986, Najīb Mahfūz (Egypt) in 1988, and Nadine Gordimer (South Africa) in 1991, are in the collections, too.

Recognized internationally for his poetry and essays, Léopold Sédar Senghor, the first president of Senegal, and several other writers (for instance, Aimé Césaire, who first used the word in print in a poem in 1937) developed the concept of *négritude*, a term used to describe that which is distinctive about African culture as found on the continent and in the diaspora. Senghor's *Anthologie de la nouvelle poésie nègre et malgache de langue française* (1948), a collection reflecting *négritude*, has been noted as a milestone in African literature, influencing other authors particularly in francophone and lusophone countries.

OPPOSITE. A hand-illuminated photographic detail from a map of Ethiopia drawn in 1923 shows Haile Selassie (1892–1974), who reigned as emperor of Ethiopia from 1930 to 1974 and who once owned the map. *(Geography and Map Division)*

Recipient of the first prize for novelists at the World Festival of Negro Arts held in Dakar, Senegal, in 1967, Senegalese writer Sembene Ousmane (b. 1923) is also recognized as one of Africa's leading cinematographers. His films are found in the Motion Picture, Broadcasting, and Recorded Sound Division; his writings are in the General Collections of the Library. *(Motion Picture, Broadcasting, and Recorded Sound Division)*

African literature has been made into television dramas and films. For example, Chinua Achebe's popular *Things Fall Apart* (1958), describing life in Nigeria, was made into a thirteen-episode television miniseries in 1990 and now can be viewed in the Library's Motion Picture, Broadcasting, and Recorded Sound Division.

From time to time, outstanding African authors are invited to the Library's Recording Laboratory, of the Motion Picture, Broadcasting, and Recorded Sound Division to read from their work and comment on it for the ongoing *Archive of World Literature on Tape*, accessible in the Recorded Sound Reference Center and Listening Facility. In addition, the archive includes material that was intended for broadcast as part of the Voice of America radio program "Conversations with African Writers," hosted by Lee Nichols. Some of these interviews have been published in *Conversations with African Writers: Interviews with Twenty-six African Authors* (1981).

In addition to the poets, novelists, and dramatists mentioned above, the African continent has continued to produce many outstanding nonfiction writers whose works the Library of Congress collects. The historian Mahmoûd Kâti (1468–1593), also known as Maḥmūd K't ibn al-Mutawakkil K't, is highly regarded for his *Tārīkh al-fattāsh*, a collection of stories and legends about the Ghana empire dating back to the seventh century A.D. Building on the work of his teacher, Ahmad ibn Ahmad Baba (1556–1627), who was from Tombouctou, an important trade center on the caravan routes across the Sahara, 'Abd al-Rāḥmān ibn 'Abd Allāh al-Sa'dī (1596–1656?) describes nine hundred years of African history in his *Tārīkh al-Sūdān*. More recent historians include Joseph Ki-Zerbo of Burkina Faso, who in addition to writing many articles and histories of Africa, served as an editor of UNESCO's eight-volume *General History of Africa* (1981–91). Although a physics professor at the Senegalese national university, Cheikh Anta Diop has become best-known for his writings on the origin of man and the history of ancient African civilizations, many of which have been translated from French into English.

The examples described above illustrate the rich treasury of creative expression, intellectual challenge, and cultural diversity preserved in the Library's Africana collections.

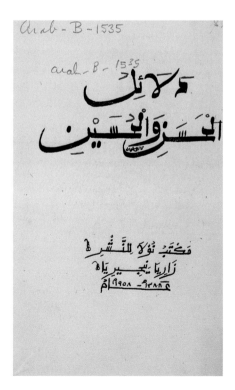 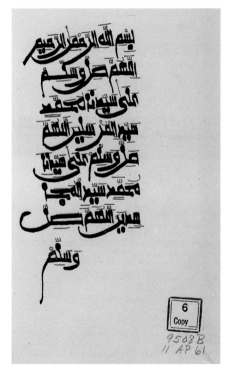

Dalā'il al-Ḥasan wa-al-Ḥusayn (1958), an Islamic prayer book from Zaria, Nigeria, offers a beautiful modern example of handwritten Arabic calligraphy used to write an African language. *(Near East Section)*

African Peoples' Encounters With Others

Throughout the centuries, peoples born in the area known as sub-Saharan Africa have interacted on many levels with peoples from elsewhere. The Library of Congress Africana collections are rich in primary documents, facsimiles, and secondary sources in a variety of languages and formats that describe these experiences. Texts, maps, visual images, artifacts, and recordings document the observations of non-Africans as they traveled to parts of the continent and of Africans who encountered them willingly or under coercion. These materials also describe the resistance and adaptation of Africans to the cultural and political onslaught of non-Africans. Diverse resources are available to study the development of commercial and diplomatic relations; the creation and dissolution of colonial governments; and the reestablishment of sovereign nations.

Some of the earliest writings mentioning African peoples describe the relations between the peoples of the Horn of Africa and peoples living in Egypt, on the Arabian peninsula, or in India, where an active trading network across the Red Sea and the Indian Ocean was already well established in ancient times. In West Africa, kingdoms such as Ghana, Mali, and Songhai engaged in trans-Saharan trade with North Africa as early as A.D. 300, flourishing particularly in the Middle Ages. The Library has many accounts of these historic encounters in the original languages—Chinese, Arabic, and others—of the observers as well as in various translations.

Travelers to and from Africa, whether they were traders, government or military officers, or people returning to Africa after the diaspora, have produced descriptions of their experiences. In the Manuscript Division, the Naval Historical Foundation collection and the Peter Force papers contain the records, correspondence, logbooks, and maritime reports of many American naval and merchant seamen who sailed the coasts of Africa and described the social, political, and economic conditions observed. In the same division are found the papers of other American travelers, such as those of the abolitionist, diplomat, journalist, and orator Frederick Douglass (1817?-1895), who traveled to Africa in 1845–47 and 1886–87. The papers of W. E. B. Du Bois (1868–1963), author, educator, and historian, describe his travels in Africa and are available on microfilm.

African travelers to the United States and other countries have described their experiences and views of those areas. Recent examples include Prince Bamgbola Akinsanya's *America!: Candid Impressions of an African: A Comparison of Two Cultures* (1992) and H. Martin Th. Kayamba's *An African in Europe* (1948), both housed in the General Collections.

Some of the writings of Africans captured in slavery reside in the Library's

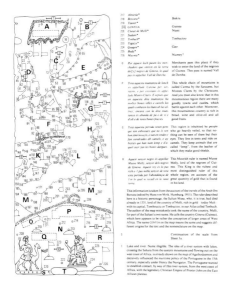

ABOVE AND OPPOSITE. This map shows the trip to Mecca made in A.D. 1324 by the fabulously wealthy king Mansa Musa (reigned, 1312?–37) of the Mali Empire. With the map is an explanation of some of the symbols it uses. This facsimile of the Catalan Atlas, probably by Abraham Crèsques (d. 1387), edited and with commentary by Georges Grosjean, was published as *Mapamundi, the Catalan Atlas of the Year 1375* (Dietikon-Zurich: Urs Graf; sole distributor in the United States and Canada: Abaris Books, 1978). (*Copyright © 1978 by Urs Graf, Publisher, GmbH, 1978. Used by permission of Abaris Books.*) (*Geography and Map Division*)

OPPOSITE TOP. "A New Map of the Coast of Guinea from Cape Mount to Iacquin" appeared in William Smith's *Thirty Different Drafts of Guinea* (not before 1727), which illustrates the fierce competition among the Dutch, English, and Portuguese along the west coast of Africa in areas they called the Grain, the Ivory, the Gold, and the Slave Coasts. The volume includes diagrams of the forts they built, landscapes, and pictorial information that sheds light on the slave trade. (*Rare Book and Special Collections Division*)

OPPOSITE BOTTOM. "Isle de Madagascar ou de St. Laurens" is by the French geographer Nicolas Sanson, whose *L'Affriqve; en plvsieurs cartes novvelles, et exactes; & en divers traitez de geographie, et d'histoire* (1656), is one of the earliest atlases in the Library of Congress devoted exclusively to Africa. Sanson includes extensive descriptions of the continent and its peoples. (*Geography and Map Division*)

RIGHT. Johann Theodor de Bry (1561–1623?) in his *India Orientalis pars VI. Veram et historicam descriptionem avrifeie* (1604) provides an excellent example of the type of book published in Europe about the African continent to astound and amaze Europeans in the seventeenth century. Pictured here in profile are eight men and eight women of Benin whose hair styles resemble some still popular today in Africa as well as in the diaspora. (*Rare Book and Special Collections Division*)

Rare Book and Special Collections Division. Among them are first and subsequent editions of the *Thoughts and Sentiments on the Evil and Wicked Traffic of the Slavery and Commerce of the Human Species* (1787) by Ottobah Cugoano (ca. 1745–ca. 1790), said to be from Ghana originally. Nigerian Olaudah Equiano (ca. 1745–ca. 1802) wrote his autobiographical *Interesting Narrative,* which was published in 1789. One of the earliest African American poets, Phillis Wheatley, born in the Senegal River valley in about 1753, is known for her *Poems on Various Subjects, Religious and Moral* (1773), part of the John Davis Batchelder Collection.

One of the largest Africana collections in the Library is that of the American Colonization Society. The finding aid *The American Colonization Society: A Register of Its Records in the Library of Congress* (1979) guides the researcher through these documents, which number 190,000 pieces. Formed in 1817 and dissolved in 1964, the society was established to facilitate the repatriation of African Americans back to Africa, first in Sierra Leone and then principally in Liberia.

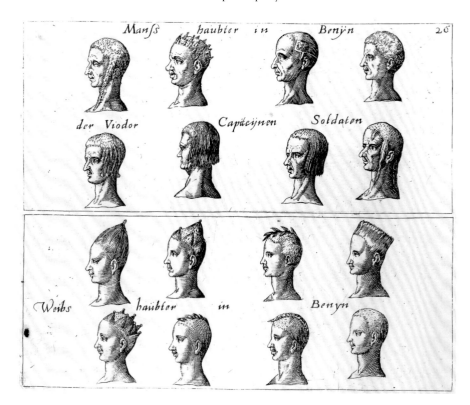

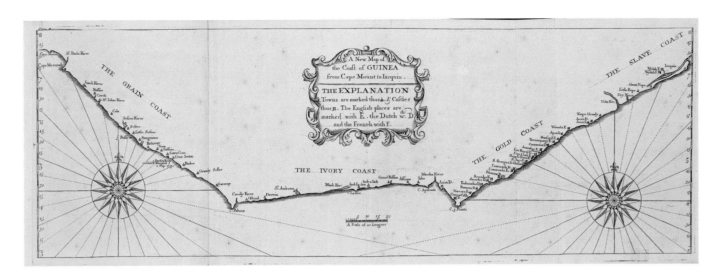

A New Map of
the Coast of GUINEA
from Cape Mount to Iacquin.

THE EXPLANATION
Towns are marked thus ⚬ ʄ Castles
thus ⊓. The English places are
marked with E. the Dutch w. D.
and the French with F.

THE GRAIN COAST

THE SLAVE COAST

THE GOLD COAST

THE IVORY COAST

A Scale of 20 Leagues

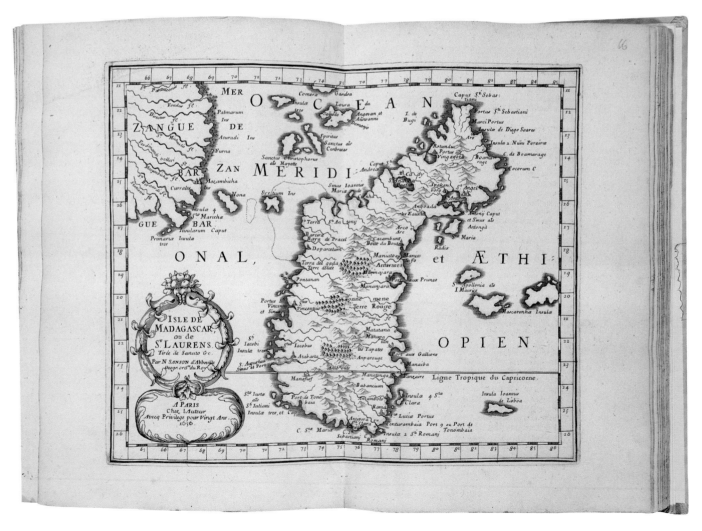

MER DE ZANGUE BARZAN GUE BAR

OCEAN MERIDI ONAL, et ÆTHI OPIEN

ISLE DE
MADAGASCAR
ou de
St LAURENS
Tirée de Sanuto &c.
Par N. SANSON d'Abbeville
Geogr. ord. du Roy.

A PARIS
Chez l'Auteur
Avecq Privilege pour Vingt Ans.
1656

Ligne Tropique du Capricorne.

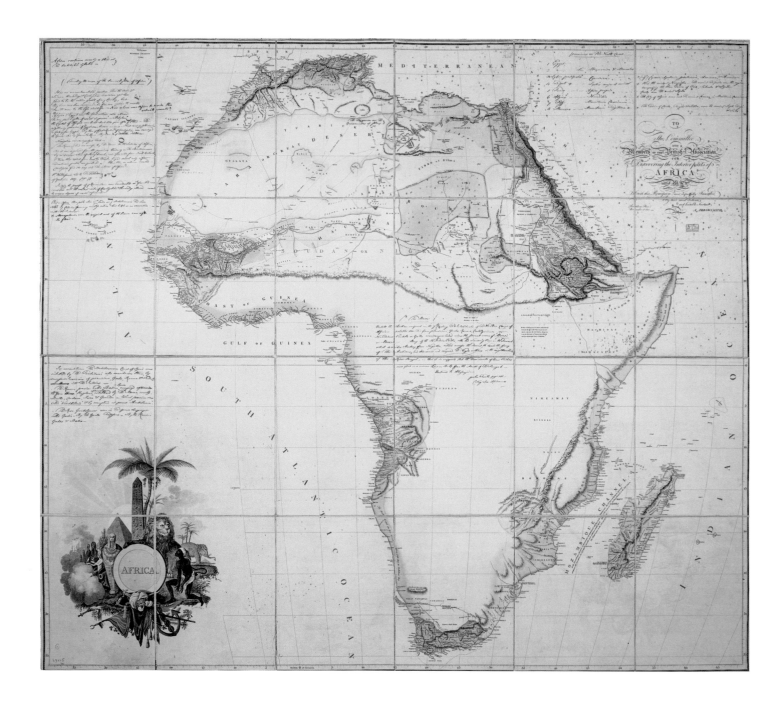

The ACS archives included photographs and postcards (now housed in the Prints and Photographs Division); correspondence, internal reports, and other official documents (in the Manuscript Division); and maps (in the Geography and Map Division). Some of these materials are available electronically through the Internet as part of the American Memory project accessible from the Library's Web site. Materials that complement the American Colonization Society collection include Daniel Coker's journal of 1821 (housed in the Manuscript Division), which records daily events at the society's colony at Fourah Bay, Sierra Leone, where Coker served as its agent.

Consisting of nearly four hundred pamphlets, the Daniel Murray Pamphlet Collection, housed in the Rare Book and Special Collections Division, has also been partially digitized and is accessible on the Internet. Daniel A. P. Murray was a valued Library employee for many years who spent a lifetime assembling his personal collection of mostly African American studies materials, which was bequeathed to the Library after his death in 1926. Among the digitized pamphlets is *The Foulahs of Central Africa, and the African Slave Trade* (1843).

The early history of African-European government relations is documented in the work of Jacobus Philippus Bergomensis (1434–1520). His *Supplementum chronicarum* (1486) contains a partial account of the treatise written by Giovanni da Carignano based on interviews Carignano supposedly conducted with members of the diplomatic mission sent by King Wadem Ar'ad of Ethiopia to the papal court in Avignon in A.D. 1306. In several anthologies and translations in the Library's collections, the correspondence exchanged between Afonso I, king of the Congo (ca. 1456–ca. 1541) whose prebaptismal name was Mvemba Nsinga, and Manuel I, king of Portugal (1469–1521), is available.

In 1884–85, the Berlin Conference brought together delegates from Austria, Belgium, Denmark, France, Great Britain, Italy, Luxumbourg, Netherlands, Portugal, Prussia, Russia, Spain, Sweden, and Turkey to discuss the competitive interests of each for colonies in Africa. The map of Africa soon reflected the agreements made at this conference and ushered in the colonial period of African history. The establishment of colonial administrations generated many documents and publications. The African Section has prepared a series of guides to official publications of these governments and to those of the subsequent independent nations (see "Selected Library of Congress Publications on Africa").

In this same period, many Catholic and Protestant missionaries were sent to the continent to convert and educate the African peoples and to inculcate Eurocentric culture in them. Microfilmed archives of some of these societies are held

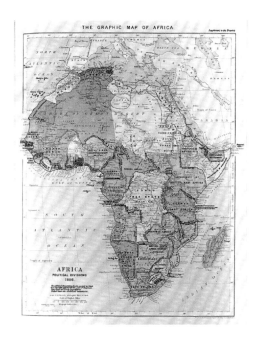

OPPOSITE. Aaron Arrowsmith's *To the Committee and Members of the British Association for Discovering the Interior Parts of Africa This Map Is with Their Permission Most Respectfully Inscribed* (1802) and, ABOVE, Edward Stanford's *Stanford's Library Map of Africa; New Edition* (1896), drawn respectively at the beginning and at the end of the nineteenth century, graphically show the results of a century of European exploration and colonization. Arrowsmith, the leading nineteenth-century British map publisher, strove to produce maps with the most accurate information possible, most of the data coming directly from explorers and travelers. Stanford is known for his publication of maps widely used in schools and libraries. (*Geography and Map Division*)

by the Library, for example, the *IMC-CBMS Missionary Archives* (1977), a collection of about 1,850 microfiches concerning the International Missionary Council and the Conference of British Missionary Societies. These archives cover the period from 1910 to 1945 and are available in the Microform Reading Room.

The resistance of Africans to the cultural and political assault of the Europeans is also documented in the Library's collections. *The Mombasa Rising against the Portuguese, 1631: From Sworn Evidence* (1980) presents in English translation the "Diocesis Goanae Processus martyrum de Mombassa," a record of the court of inquiry held by the diocese of Mombasa to ascertain whether those who died during the rebellion were martyrs and eligible for canonization as saints. The testimonies of eyewitnesses give the historian views of the confrontation between Islam and Christianity and between African and European political powers. Their accounts provide an insight into the social and cultural interactions of peoples living in the Mombasa, Kenya, area of Eastern Africa in the seventeenth century.

The Library offers researchers a dazzling array of graphic resources that portray the ways in which Africans were viewed by others and how Africans saw themselves and other peoples. These materials include drawings reproduced as etchings and lithographs in books, newspapers, or periodicals, as individual images such as photographs and daguerreotypes, or as films and videotapes.

In David Killinray and Andrew Robert's essay, "An Outline History of Photography in Africa (to c. 1940)," in *Photographs as Sources for African History* (1988), it is noted that "In South Africa, studios were established in the Cape in the late 1840s and 1850s.... In Luanda [Angola], a studio opened around 1863. During the 1880s there were at least seven studios in Freetown [Sierra Leone] run by black photographers, and by this time there were also studios in Accra and Zanzibar" (p. 10). *The Red Book of West Africa: Historical and Descriptive, Commercial and Industrial Facts, Figures, & Resources* (1920) contains the photographs of the following photographers: George S. Da Costa of Nigeria; N. Wlawin Holm who was born in Accra, had a studio in Lagos, and was the first Nigerian member of the Royal Photographic Society of Great Britain; and Alphonso and Arthur Lisk-Carew of Sierra Leone. The volume claimed to be "the first of its kind ever issued on West Africa, also the most profusely illustrated."

From the 1870s through the 1930s, stereograph companies deposited more than 250,000 stereograph cards for copyright in the Library of Congress, of which approximately 2,500 show African scenes. Arranged geographically in file cabinets, these stereographs show details of life in various parts of the continent, such as the court in session in a courtroom filled with officials, audience, and witnesses pictured in *A Native Court in Ujiji, Tanganyika Territory, Africa* (P&P stereo. no. 20767).

Other photographic collections include the Royal Commonwealth Society's RCS *Photograph Collection: Africa* (1985–87), found in the Microform Reading Room, consisting of 208 microfiches which document the colonization and administration of former British colonies in Africa. The photograph albums of Frank G. Carpenter (1855–1924), the American author and journalist who traveled all around the world during a period of over thirty years, are housed in the Prints and Photographs Division. Carpenter wrote about and photographed many African countries—including Uganda, Rhodesia, Mozambique, and the Union of South Africa.

OPPOSITE. Labeled "King Kobina of Elmina, Ghana" (ca. 1890s), this photograph is one in a collection dated 1890–1910. Here the royal court is portrayed in traditional dress surrounding the king. In the same collection is a photograph showing some of the same people, but wearing Western clothing and posed more informally under some trees. (*Frank and Frances Carpenter Collection. Prints and Photographs Division*)

Flags have been used since the seventeenth century by the Fanti (or Fante) in the coastal areas of Ghana to identify their military companies, called Asafo, which serve as political, cultural, and military advisers. The appliquéd symbols on the flags may identify a company by name, number, and geographic location, using imagery illustrating the power and glory of the unit. This example is found in an exhibit catalog of African textiles, *Daiei Hakubutsukan shozohin ni yoru Afurika no senshoku* (Kyoto, 1991). *(Copyright © The National Museum of Modern Art, Kyoto, 1991) (General Collections)*

Early Motion Pictures: The Paper Print Collection in the Library of Congress (Washington: Library of Congress, 1985) describes two moving pictures apparently filmed on location in Africa, although the country is not designated for either. *Military Drill of Kikuyu Tribes and Other Native Ceremonies* was deposited for copyright on July 4, 1914, and *Paul J. Rainey's African Hunt* on April 22, 1912.

The Library has the world's largest collection of maps and atlases, including many of interest to the Africanist. From ancient hand-drawn charts to the latest satellite surveys, the Geography and Map Division houses more than 150,000 maps and atlases on Africa, offering diverse types of information such as political and geographic divisions, environmental conditions, and ethnological data. For example, the collection includes the 1477 Bologna edition of Claudius Ptolemy's *Geography*, based on Ptolemy's writings of about A.D. 150 and on what was known from Arab and European writers up to 1477.

Maps are often found in travel accounts. A map of West Africa drawn for the benefit of a European traveler at the command of Muhammad Bello, sultan of Sokoto (d. 1837), was published in 1826 in *Narrative of Travels and Discoveries in Northern and Central Africa, in the Years 1822, 1823, and 1824* by Dixon Denham, Hugh Clapperton, and Walter Oudney, who were travelers and explorers in that region.

The historic complexity of the encounters between African peoples and others has produced a multiplicity of materials. The Library's Africana collections offer researchers a wide selection of resources reflecting a variety of approaches to documenting these interactions.

For a number of works, the Library owns both a set of photographs that was compiled for publication and the published book itself. *Introducing West Africa,* issued by the Great Britain Colonial Office and the Central Office of Information in several editions from 1944 to 1955, included a photograph whose original legend read in part, "The West African has won considerable repute for his skill as a craftsman.... Today wood carving is chief among West African crafts." Promotional works such as this were issued by colonial governments to encourage tourism and settlement in their colonies. *(Prints and Photographs Division)*

Contemporary African States

THE LIBRARY OF CONGRESS has sought to collect materials that reflect the political, economic, social, and technological developments in contemporary sub-Saharan Africa. Materials published in Africa during the last thirty years offer scholars of contemporary African states unparalleled resources for study at the Library. Publishers include government ministries, government printing offices, research institutes, banks, nongovernmental organizations, commercial publishers, courts, university departments, and libraries.

In its various reading rooms, the Library of Congress offers information in such diverse formats as multivolume encyclopedias, sound recordings, books, computer disks, press releases, and government documents. For example, in the Newspaper and Current Periodical Room, the Library receives newspapers from capital cities of all the African states and from many major African cities as well. Approximately 6,000 current Africana periodicals arrive regularly, providing scholars with timely information.

Researchers are offered a wealth of national, provincial, and municipal documents issued by African governments, which, in many countries serve as the principal publishers. Materials from national governments range from presidential speeches, tourist brochures, annual reports of government agencies or ministries, statistical abstracts, and budgets to broad policy statements or multivolume, long-range development plans. The Library selectively acquires provincial or state and municipal publications, which often prove invaluable for researchers studying local community government and living conditions. For example, the Nairobi City Commission (formerly called the City Council) issues *Minutes of Proceedings of the Commission* for various time periods that include reports from city committees, such as the Housing Development Committee, the Education and Social Services Committee, and the Public Health Committee, as well as information about government contracts.

By using more than one format to present information, governments reach a wider audience. For example, Réunion has produced the video *Budget 90,* in which a government official explains specific aspects of the 1990 budget. To assist in AIDS education, the Malawi AIDS Control Programme has produced *Tinkanena: A Film about AIDS for Std 7 + 8* (1992).

Besides the videos described above, the Motion Picture, Broadcasting, and Recorded Sound Division has additional resources helpful to the student of contemporary Africa. For example, the video *Talking Back,* described on its container as "Voices from Southern Africa" (1994), features interviews with development workers and others concerning multiparty elections and World

OPPOSITE. *Africa* (September 1997) is an example of the helpful, widely distributed low-cost maps issued by the Central Intelligence Agency (CIA) of the U.S. government. The CIA produces maps regularly to reflect changes in geographical names and boundaries. As government documents, they are not protected by copyright and are therefore popular for use and reproduction by others. (*Geography and Map Division*)

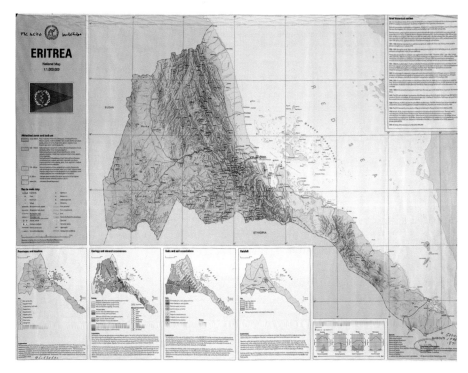

RIGHT AND OPPOSITE. Eritrea is the newest sub-Saharan African country to be recognized as a sovereign nation, which it was as of May 24, 1991. The production of the official map *Eritrea: National Map* (1995) illustrates the importance accorded by a new nation to establishing its national boundaries. Serving equally important needs, *The State of Eritrea: A Satellite Image Map* (1994?) was issued by the Eritrean Ministry of Energy, Mines, and Water Resources based on fourteen electronic images from a U.S. Landsat satellite, 1985–89. The maps monitor seasonal changes in vegetation, and record geological features, mountains, deserts, reefs, and the courses of streams and rivers. (*Courtesy Embassy of the State of Eritrea*) (*Geography and Map Division*)

Bank and International Monetary Fund economic solutions. Recordings of television news programs such as *Nightline* and its June 13, 1990, broadcast *Liberia Civil War* also offer unique combinations of research material.

A department within the Library of Congress, the Law Library has extensive collections of laws, regulations, gazettes, constitutions, international agreements, and unofficial legal material such as compilations of laws, digests, dictionaries, and encyclopedias for African countries. African law is generally defined as customary (traditional), colonial (based on the legal system of the former colonial power, if any), or sovereign. All of these types are represented in the Library's collections. Usually, laws, announcements, and decisions pertaining to government agencies are published in official gazettes or, in francophone countries, *journaux officiels*. The Library's gazette collections are excellent.

The depth and continued growth of the Law Library's holdings are remarkable. The Republic of South Africa, for instance, held its first democratic elections in which all of its citizens could participate in April 1994. Many use this date to mark the beginning of a new era, with the disassembly of the apartheid system.

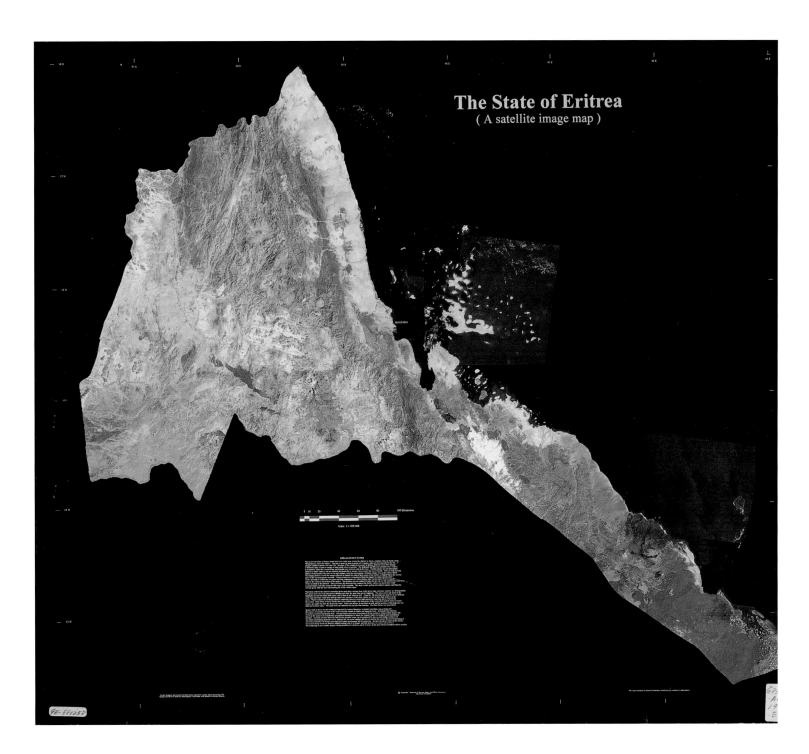

The State of Eritrea
(A satellite image map)

Photographs issued by Photo Information, Côte d'Ivoire (1959), present typical scenes of rural tranquility or small town bustle which may be found throughout the African continent. Taken in the northern part of Côte d'Ivoire, the photo information shot above depicts an informal group of men ranging in age talking under a baobab, a tree common to the Sahel region. Shown at right is a busy traditional market day in Agbouille, Côte d'Ivoire. *(Prints and Photographs Division).*

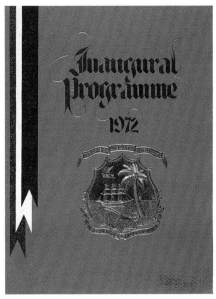

ABOVE. A souvenir program from the first inaugural ceremonies of President William Richard Tolbert Jr., twentieth president (1971–80) of the Republic of Liberia, is an example of the rare political ephemera available to the researcher at the Library. (*African Section Pamphlet Collection*)

LEFT. This aerial view of downtown Nairobi (ca. 1985), the capital of Kenya, dispels the misconception that life in sub-Saharan Africa is lived solely in rural, underdeveloped areas. The major cities of African countries look similar to those found anywhere, and have many of the same problems—one being rush hour traffic congestion, which sometimes occurs four, not just two times a day as in the United States. (*Photo courtesy of the Embassy of Kenya*) (*African Section Pamphlet Collection*)

In many countries anti-apartheid activists and sympathizers launched numerous solidarity campaigns to provide moral and material support to the liberation of South Africa and Namibia. Posters were issued to gain support for these movements. (*African Section Poster Collection*)

As of December 1997, the Law Library had added 117 monographs published from 1994 through 1997 concerning South African law to its collections. Also as part of a continuing effort to document trends in legal theory and revisions to established systems, the Library acquired the two-volume report of the *Malawi Legal and Judicial Reform Task Force* (1996) and maintains a subscription to the *Annual Report* of the Women and Law in Southern Africa Research Project, published in Harare, Zimbabwe.

While treaties themselves are located in the Law Library, collections of papers housed in the Manuscript Division document African diplomatic history and twentieth-century U.S.–African relations. The papers of American diplomats offer the opportunity to study the development of official links between African nations and the United States. For example, the papers of Ambassadors Hugh and Mabel Smythe number more than 34,000 items and include materials from Mabel Smythe's service as U.S. ambassador in Cameroon. Bequeathed to the Library in 1984, the papers (1925–82) of Rayford W. Logan (1897–1982), a historian and educator, include correspondence, diaries, and other materials documenting his interests and involvement in the Pan-African movement of the 1920s and 1930s and his meetings with African leaders such as Kwame Nkrumah of Ghana and Nnamdi Azikiwe of Nigeria. Materials in the Bayard Rustin papers (1942–87, most dated 1963–80) concern Rustin's visits to West Africa in the 1950s when this civil rights leader and social reformer helped organize nonviolent resistance campaigns against colonialism and nuclear weapons. They recount his observations on the elections in Zimbabwe and reveal his interest in issues affecting Ethiopian refugees in Somalia and Sudan.

Extensive holdings of materials produced by nongovernmental and international organizations may be found in various divisions of the Library. Some are in the General Collections; others are housed in the African Section's Pamphlet Collection or dispersed to custodial divisions according to their format. For example, *African Development Indicators,* issued annually by the United Nations Development Programme and the World Bank, is available in a print edition and on a computer disk. Archives and collections of organizations such as the *Records of the American Committee on Africa*, consisting of fifty-one microfilm reels housed in the Manuscript Division of which forty-five are correspondence and subject files on South Africa, 1952–85, document the roles of these organizations in African affairs.

Interest in Africa has increased markedly since 1960, with a resultant increase in the number of publications about the continent. In the case of U.S. government publications, for example, *The United States and Sub-Saharan Africa: Guide to U.S.*

TOM MBOYA, M.L.C.
(General Secretary Kenya Federation of Labour)
NAIROBI AREA

ALVI HOUSE, VICTORIA STREET

Cables: 'INTCONFED' NAIROBI.
P.O. Box 10818
N A I R O B I
K E N Y A .

Phone 21838

Ref. No. ....

Date .... 12th June, 195...

Dear Brother Randolph

     Our trial is now over and I have xxxxxxxxxxx to inform you that on the first count we were all convicted and fined £75 each. The Magistrate dismissed the charge of conspiracy to commit a misdemeanour. Our application for compensation for a vexatious charge relating to the second was refused.

     I take this opportunity to thank all our friends and sympathisers who so willingly, readily and generously rallied to our side at our hour of need. I am personally indebted to you for the interest you have xxxxxx shown in our struggle.

     May I also here state very categorically our complete satisfaction with our Senior Counsel Mr. D.N.Pritt. Q.C. and Junior Counsel Mr. A.R.Kapila whose efficient and competent handling of the case was beyond doubt.

     In our struggle such obstacles may come from time to time, but we have faith and confidence in our people and country and in the inevitable triumph of justice, oppression and suppression. We are deeply committed to the course for democracy and human liberties and this we hope to establish for all peoples in our country no matter what their colour or racial origin may be.

     I hope that you and your friends and organisation will always continue to give us the moral and other support that we may need in this struggle from time to time.

Yours Sincerely,

T. Mboya
TOM MBOYA, M.L.C.

AFRICAN-AMERICAN STUDENTS FOUNDATION, INC.

SUITE 4710 70 PINE STREET
NEW YORK 5, NEW YORK

UNITED STATES OF AMERICA
PRESIDENT
WILLIAM X. SCHEINMAN
VICE-PRESIDENT
GEORGE HOUSER
VICE-PRESIDENT
FRANK C. MONTERO
SECRETARY-TREASURER
JOHN H. BALL

AFRICAN ASSOCIATES
HON. TOM MBOYA
MEMBER, KENYA LEGISLATIVE COUNCIL
KARIUKI K. NJIIRI
MEMBER, KENYA EDUCATION DEPARTMENT

August 24, 1959

Mr. Philip Randolph
217 W. 125th St.,
New York 27, N. Y.

Dear Mr. Randolph:

We are writing you about an urgent matter which we feel confident will appeal to your sense of fair play.

Recently, twenty-eight year old Tom Mboya, the brilliant young African leader came to America to interpret the aspiration of the African people for freedom. As Chairman of the All African Peoples Conference, Tom Mboya's voice and influence extend far outside his native Kenya.

In his whirlwind tour from coast to coast he dramatized the need for higher education of the many young Kenyans for whom opportunities are non-existent under the repressive colonial system. In Kenya today higher education is not available to Africans.

The response to Tom's appeal was with typical American generosity. From over forty institutions of higher education - including Harvard, Georgetown, University of California, Michigan State College, University of Hawaii, Howard University - eighty-one scholarships have been offered. The students have already been carefully chosen and are fully prepared. This will be the largest number of students ever to come from Africa at one time.

In their own country, in a spirit of self help, African tribes and families have raised money to help bear their share. But because of the great distance - almost 8,000 miles from Kenya to New York - transportation cost is far beyond their resources.

Tom Mboya has appealed to us for help. We have undertaken to charter an airplane which is scheduled to depart from Nairobi on September 7th. This charter will substantially reduce transportation costs and insure that the students will arrive in the United States on time to leave for college campuses.

The total cost of this project is $39,000. We have personally pledged part of this sum but we cannot do it alone.

Will you respond generously to this urgent appeal by sending to us, today, your check payable to the African-American Students Foundation, Inc., to help with project Airlift-Africa. We are sure your generous response will give you deep satisfaction.

Yours sincerely,

Harry Belafonte   *Jackie Robinson*   *Sidney Poitier*
Harry Belafonte   Jackie Robinson   Sidney Poitier
AUG 25 REC'D

Official Documents and Government-Sponsored Publications on Africa, 1785–1975 (1978), which covered the entire continent, cited 8,827 U.S. government publications published during a 190-year period. Its sequel, covering only five years, 1976–80, and only sub-Saharan Africa, listed 5,047 items.

    With its vast, multimedia, multilingual Africana collections, the Library of Congress offers researchers unequaled opportunities to study contemporary sub-Saharan Africa. Knowledge of law, diplomacy, and government can be pursued through the materials that make up the Library's holdings.

Letters from the records of the Brotherhood of Sleeping Car Porters, 1920–68, which number more than 41,000 items, exemplify the importance of the links between African leaders and students and the African American community as well as the American labor movement. *(Manuscript Division)*

ABOVE. The original poster entitled "Young Tigrinya Woman" (1993–94?) is a photograph printed on fabric. It is one of a set of four art reproduction posters from Eritrea, a country which became independent on May 24, 1991. (*African Section Poster Collection*)

LEFT. Nongovernmental organizations provide rich sources of information in a myriad of formats—written and visual. This is one of fifty-six photographs in the collection *Documentary of the Effect of a Five-Year Drought on the People of the Sahelian Zone of West Africa (Mauritania, Mali, Niger, Senegal, Upper Volta, and Chad)* issued in 1973 by the Food and Agriculture Organization for a United Nations photographic exhibit on the drought. (*Photography by M. Tzovaras/VMB*) (*Prints and Photographs Division*)

A Note to Researchers

The African and Middle Eastern Division Reading Room (AMED) is the principal gateway to the Africana treasures of the Library of Congress. Here in the atmosphere of a nineteenth-century reading room, the researcher finds a browsing rack of recent Africana periodicals, a seventeen-hundred-item reference collection, and electronic resources, including public access to the Internet. Because Africana materials are spread throughout the three Capitol Hill buildings of the Library of Congress in various reading rooms and custodial divisions, identifying individual items appropriate to specific research needs may be challenging.

Researchers are encouraged to begin their visit to the Library in the African and Middle Eastern Division. The reading room is located on the second floor of the Library of Congress Thomas Jefferson Building (room LJ220) and offers a comfortable place to study, expert assistance by specialists, and a reference collection of basic resources. With the assistance of an African Section specialist— knowledgeable about both the collections and specific regions of the continent— the researcher may construct a methodology that enables him or her to get the most benefit out of a visit to the world's largest library. One-on-one consultations or group briefings may be arranged to give an overview of the Africana collections or to focus on specific subjects.

For more information, consult the African and Middle Eastern Division Reading Room's home page (<http://www.loc.gov/rr/amed>). Information about special-format custodial divisions such as the Manuscript Division or the Prints and Photographs Division—as well as the Library's Main Reading Room—may be found at <http://www.loc.gov>.

OPPOSITE. View of the African and Middle Eastern Reading Room where researchers are encouraged to begin their exploration of the Africana collections housed in diverse divisions of the Library.

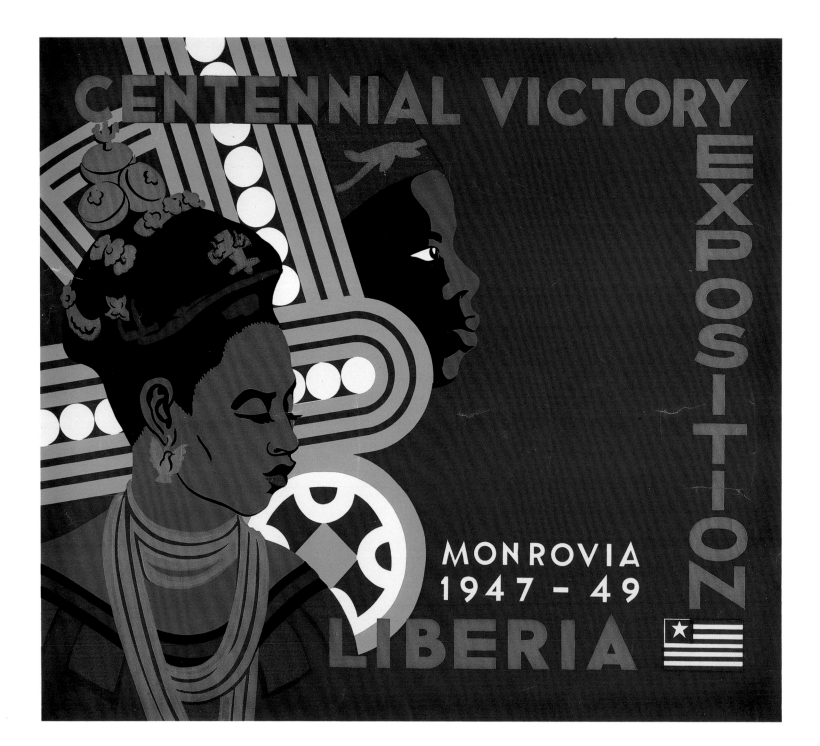

CENTENNIAL VICTORY EXPOSITION

MONROVIA
1947 - 49
LIBERIA

List of Sub-Saharan African Countries

Angola

Benin

Botswana

Burkina Faso

Burundi

Cameroon

Cape Verde

Central African Republic

Chad

Comoros

Congo (Brazzaville)

Congo (Democratic Republic)

Côte d'Ivoire

Djibouti

Equatorial Guinea

Eritrea

Ethiopia

Gabon

The Gambia

Ghana

Guinea

Guinea-Bissau

Kenya

Lesotho

Liberia

Madagascar

Malawi

Mali

Mauritania

Mauritius

Mozambique

Namibia

Niger

Nigeria

Réunion

Rwanda

Sao Tome and Principe

Senegal

Seychelles

Sierra Leone

Somalia

South Africa

Sudan

Swaziland

Tanzania

Togo

Uganda

Western Sahara

Zambia

Zimbabwe

OPPOSITE. The composition of this poster reflects both the African heritage and the unique ties between the Republic of Liberia and the United States. Liberia's national flag, the "Lone Star," reminiscent of the American "Stars and Stripes," appears in the lower right corner. The single star in the blue field representing the African continent signifies Liberia's claim to be the first African "independent republic." In the Library's custodial divisions may be found records, photographs, and maps documenting the first 100 years of the republic that grew out of the initial efforts of the American Colonization Society to repatriate freed slaves back to Africa. *(Prints and Photographs Division)*.

Selected Library of Congress Publications on Africa

OPPOSITE. In 1980, to commemorate the tenth anniversary of the opening of the Musée d'art et d'archéologie, Université de Madagascar, an exhibition of material gathered at the 1979 celebration of the Sambatra festival in Manajary was mounted. Held once every seven years in the southeastern region of Madagascar near Manakara and Manajary among the Antanbahoaka people, although today an occasion for general social, cultural, and political interaction, the traditional and continuing purpose of the weeklong Sambatra is for the mothers or the paternal aunts of male children born since the last Sambatra to bring them forward to be circumcised and presented to the community. Using the same image as the poster on its cover—an adult woman leading a small boy by the hand—the exhibition guide (found in the Library's General Collections) explains day by day each ceremony and event in both Malagasy and French. (*Prints and Photographs Division*)

Unless otherwise noted, publications listed below were published by the Library of Congress and prepared in the African Section.

Abuja: The New Federal Capital of Nigeria: A Selected List of References. 1983. 13 pp. (Africana Directions Series; AD 83-1)

Africa South of the Sahara: A Selected, Annotated List of Writings. 1963. 354 pp.

Africa South of the Sahara: Index to Periodical Literature, 1900–1970. Boston: G. K. Hall, 1971. 4 vols.

Africa South of the Sahara: Index to Periodical Literature. First Supplement. Boston: G. K. Hall, 1973. 521 pp.

Africa South of the Sahara: Index to Periodical Literature. Second Supplement. Boston: G. K. Hall, 1982. 3 vols.

Africa South of the Sahara: Index to Periodical Literature. Third Supplement. 1985. 306 pp.

African Libraries, Book Production, and Archives: A List of References. 1962. 64 pp.

African Music: A Briefly Annotated Bibliography. 1964. 55 pp.
Compiled in the Library's Music Division.

African Names and Naming Practices: A Selected List of References in English. 1977.
Reprinted from the *Library of Congress Information Bulletin*, 36 (March 2, 1977): 206–7.

African Newspapers in Selected American Libraries. 3rd ed. 1965. 135 pp.
Compiled in the Library's Serial Division.

African Newspapers in the Library of Congress. 2nd ed. 1984. 144 pp.
Compiled in the Library's Serial and Government Publications Division.

African Section in the Library of Congress. 1988. folder ([5] pp.)

Africana in the Library of Congress. [1977] folder ([5] pp.)

Agricultural Development Schemes in Sub-Saharan Africa: A Bibliography. 1963. 189 pp.
Compiled in the Library's General Reference and Bibliography Division, Bibliography and Reference Correspondence Section.

American Doctoral Dissertations on the Arab World, 1883–1968. 1970. 103 pp.
Compiled in the Library's Near East Section.

American Doctoral Dissertations on the Arab World, 1883–1974. 2nd ed. 1976. 173 pp.
Compiled in the Library's Near East Section.

American Doctoral Dissertations on the Arab World: Supplement, 1975–1981. 1983. 200 pp.
Compiled in the Library's Near East Section.

Arab-African Relations, 1973–75: A Guide. 1976. 26 pp. (Maktaba Africana Series)

Arab-World Newspapers in the Library of Congress: A List. 1980. 85 pp. (Near East Series)
Compiled in the Library's Near East Section.

SAMBATRA

Chez les Antambahoaka

TRANO FITAHIRIZANA NY VAKO-PIRENENA
MUSEE D'ART ET D'ARCHEOLOGIE
Université de Madagascar

As part of the celebration of the first decade (1974–84) of the "revolutionary transformation" of Ethiopia from empire to communist state, a number of events and related materials were produced. This colorful poster announcing the National Sports Festival sponsored by the Workers' Party of Ethiopia is one of several publications in the Library's collection produced by the Party's Propaganda and Culture Committee for the tenth anniversary. The image of runners is appropriate from a country whose long-distance runners enjoy worldwide reputations, often participating successfully in marathons such as those in Boston and New York as well as in Olympic events. The date of 1976 appearing on the poster refers to the Ethiopian calendar. (*Prints and Photographs Division*)

Botswana, Lesotho, and Swaziland: A Guide to Official Publications, 1868–1968. 1971. 84 pp.

Contemporary Amharic Creative Literature: A Guide. 1981. 43 pp. (Maktaba Afrikana Series)

East African Community: Subject Guide to Official Publications. 1976. 272 pp.

Folklore from Africa to the United States: An Annotated Bibliography. 1976. 161 pp. Compiled in the Library's Children's Literature Center.

French-Speaking Central Africa: A Guide to Official Publications in American Libraries. 1973. 314 pp.

French-Speaking West Africa: A Guide to Official Publications. 1967. 201 pp.

Ghana: A Guide to Official Publications, 1872–1968. 1969. 110 pp.

Islam in Sub-Saharan Africa: A Partially Annotated Guide. 1978. 318 pp.

Japanese-African Relations: A Selected List of References. 1988. 24 pp. (Africana Directions Series; AD 88-1)

Japanese-African Relations: A Selected List of References, no. 2. 1992. 13 pp. (Africana Directions Series; AD 92-1)

Kenya: Subject Guide to Official Publications. 1978. 423 pp.

Liberia During the Tolbert Era: A Guide. 1983. 79 pp. (Maktaba Afrikana Series).

A List of American Doctoral Dissertations on Africa. 1962. 69 pp.

Madagascar and Adjacent Islands: A Guide to Official Publications. 1965. 58 pp.

Nelson Mandela: A Selective Reading List. Reprinted from the *Library of Congress Information Bulletin,* 54 (January 9, 1995): 15–17.

Nigeria: A Guide to Official Publications. 1966. 166 pp.

Nigerian Petroleum Industry: A Guide. 1978. 66 pp. (Maktaba Africana Series)

Official Publications of British East Africa
    Part 1. *The East Africa High Commission and Other Regional Documents.* 1960. 67 pp.
    Part 2. *Tanganyika.* 1962. 134 pp.
    Part 3. *Kenya and Zanzibar.* 1962. 162 pp.
    Part 4. *Uganda.* 1963. 100 pp.

Official Publications of French Equatorial Africa, French Cameroons, and Togo, 1946–1958: A Guide. 1964. 78 pp.

Official Publications of Sierra Leone and Gambia. 1963. 92 pp.

Official Publications of Somaliland, 1941–1959. 1960. 41 pp.

Portuguese Africa: A Guide to Official Publications. 1967. 217 pp.

Recent Afro-Libyan Relations: A Selected List of References. 1981. 15 pp. (Africana Directions Series; AD 81-1)

The Rhodesias and Nyasaland: A Guide to Official Publications. 1965. 285 pp.

La Section Africaine de la Bibliothèque du Congrès. 1987. folder ([5] pp.)

Serials for African Studies. 1961. 163 pp.

Spanish-Speaking Africa: A Guide to Official Publications. 1973. 66 pp.

Sub-Saharan Africa: A Guide to Serials. 1970. 409 pp.

Tanganyika African National Union: A Guide to Publications by and about TANU. 1976. 52 pp. (Maktaba Afrikana Series)

U.S. Imprints on Sub-Saharan Africa: A Guide to Publications Cataloged at the Library of Congress. vols. 1–8 (1985–92)

Uganda: Subject Guide to Official Publications. 1977. 271 pp.

United States and Africa: Guide to U.S. Official Documents and Government-Sponsored Publications on Africa, 1785–1975. 1978. 949 pp.

United States and Sub-Saharan Africa: Guide to U.S. Official Documents and Government-Sponsored Publications on Africa, 1976–1980. 1984. 721 pp. Compiled in the Library's African and Middle Eastern Division.

United States and Canadian Publications on Africa in 1960. 1962. 98 pp.

University of Malawi Publications: A Guide. 1980. 41 pp. (Maktaba Afrikana Series)

Zanzibar's Afro-Shirazi Party, 1957–1977: A Bibliography. 1978. 20 pp. (Maktaba Afrikana Series)

Selected Writings about the Africana Collections

Duignan, Peter. *Handbook of American Resources for African studies*. [Stanford]: Hoover Institution on War, Revolution, and Peace, Stanford University, 1967. pp. 40–51.

Gosebrink, Jean E. Meeh. *African Studies Information Resources Directory*. Oxford, England: H. Zell, 1986. pp. 145–46.
"A partial revision of Peter Duignan's *Handbook of American Resources for African Studies* (1967)"

Gray, Beverly A. "Africana Acquisitions at the Library of Congress." In *Africana Resources and Collections: Three Decades of Development and Achievement: A Festschrift in Honor of Hans Panofsky*, edited by Julian W. Witherell. Metuchen, N.J.: Scarecrow Press, 1989. pp. 62–76.

Library of Congress. *Quarterly Journal of the Library of Congress*, 27, no. 3 (July 1970): 184–283.
This entire issue on Africana in the Library's collections contains articles on various materials concerning Africa written in celebration of the African Section's tenth anniversary.

South, Aloha. *Guide to Non-federal Archives and Manuscripts in the United States Relating to Africa*. London; New York: H. Zell Publishers, 1989, c1988. Vol. 1, pp. 146–339.

Zellers, Joanne M. "The Library of Congress African Section." In *African Studies: Papers Presented at a Colloquium at the British Library, 7–9 January 1985.* edited by Ilse Sternberg and Patricia M. Larby. London: The Library in association with SCOLMA, 1986. pp. 289–98.

OPPOSITE. Within two years of independence (October 1, 1960) from the United Kingdom, Nigeria, recognizing the importance of marketing its products on a global basis, hosted its first international trade fair, announced by this poster. As President Obasanjo would say of a later fair held in Lagos in 1977 at the recently constructed fair complex, "a trade fair is a market organized to promote trade, where buyers and sellers gather to transact business.... Nigeria wants to and ought to participate in the more lucrative aspect of this international trade." (*Prints and Photographs Division*)

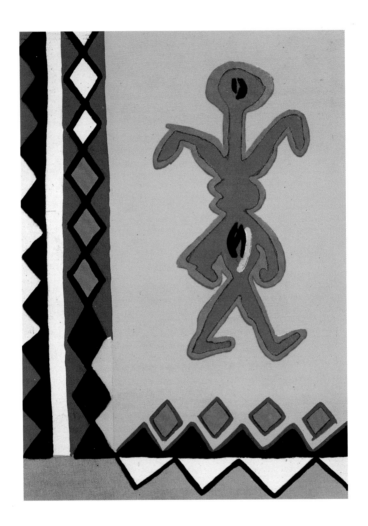

A mural painting, from a house in southern Lunda is pictured on a postcard produced for the Companhia de Diamantes
de Angola (1960s), from the collection of
the Museu do Dundo, Angola. *(Prints and
Photographs Division)*